THE
Children's
GREEN DETECTIVE GUIDE TO
CORNWALL

CONTENTS

Design **Bert Braham**

Written by **Debs Rooney**

Illustrated by **Seland Graphics & Pamela Wilson**

www.greenguides.co.uk ~ email:agenda21publishing@btclick.com

Publishers Statement
Published by Agenda 21 Publishing Ltd Unit 2 Orchard Business Centre Salfords Surrey RH1 5EL
First edition © text and illustrations Agenda 21 Publishing Ltd

Printed on 100% recycled paper

LAND BEYOND ENGLAND

Cornwall is a very special area of England, full of myths and legends with lots of interesting things to do and places to see.

When you look at a map of the United Kingdom, Cornwall is at the very bottom in the left hand corner.

As you crossed from Devon you might have seen the Cornish Coat of Arms welcoming you to this area.

COAT OF ARMS

The Cornish Coat of Arms shows a fisherman and a tin miner.

These trades were once Cornwall's two main industries.

If you look carefully at the miner's hat you will see a candle that was used to light the rock face where he would be working.

THE SHIELD

The shield has 15 gold balls or circles that are thought to show the ransom raised in Cornwall for the release of the Duke of Cornwall.

He was captured by the Saracens during the Crusades in the 14th century and was so grateful to the Cornish people for paying his ransom that he showed these 15 coins on his Coat of Arms.

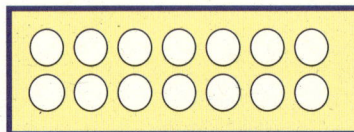

LAND'S END

The very tip of Cornwall is called Land's End, because that's exactly what it is! The next land mass is America which is over 4,827 kilometres away.

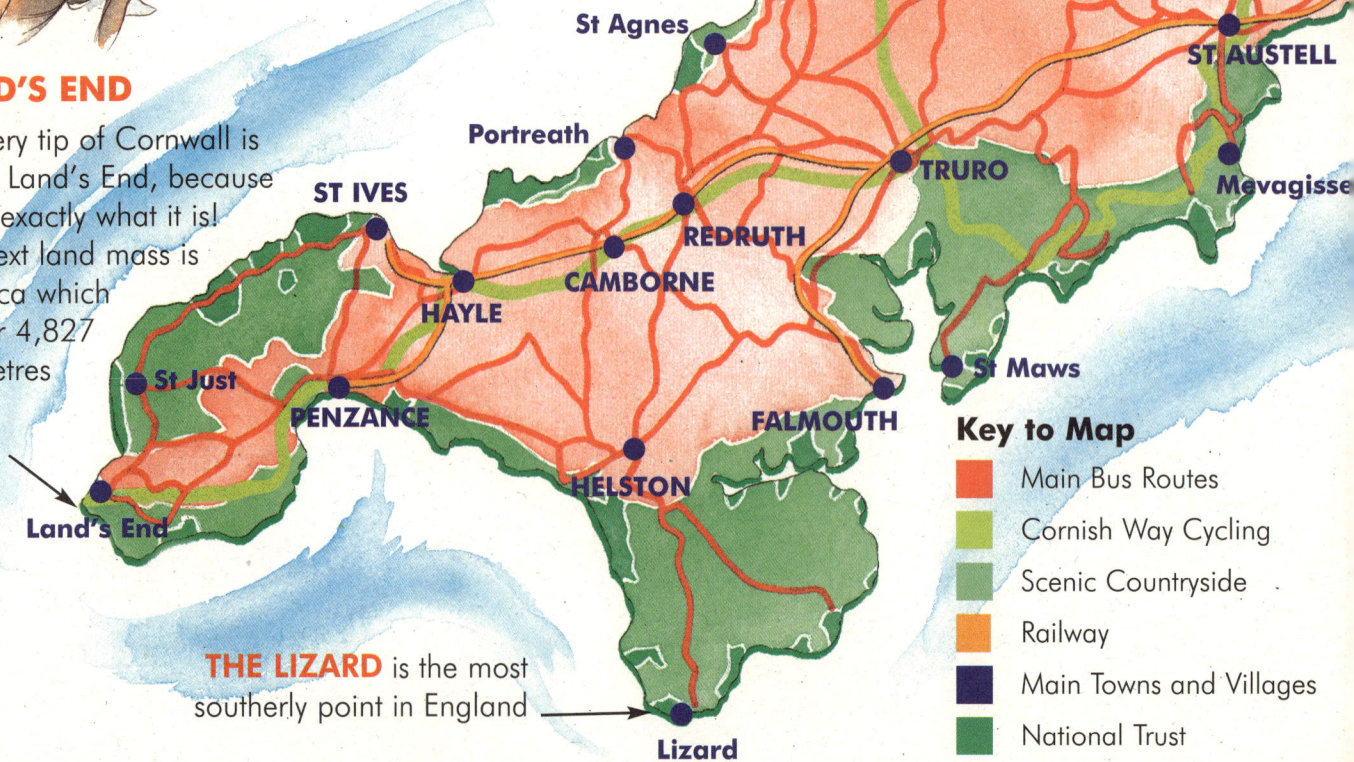

Every time you see one of these Coats of Arms colour in one of the coins.

THE LIZARD is the most southerly point in England

Key to Map

- Main Bus Routes
- Cornish Way Cycling
- Scenic Countryside
- Railway
- Main Towns and Villages
- National Trust

Boscas
Tintagel
Polzeath
PADSTOW
WADEBRIDGE
BODM
NEWQUAY
St Agnes
ST AUSTELL
Portreath
TRURO
Mevagisse
ST IVES
REDRUTH
CAMBORNE
HAYLE
St Maws
St Just
PENZANCE
FALMOUTH
Land's End
HELSTON
Lizard

IS CORNWALL?

HOW FAR HAVE YOU TRAVELLED?

Find the town or city closest to where you live to find out roughly how far you will have travelled to get to Cornwall.

KMS to PENZANCE FROM:		
Glasgow	(A)	899kms
Edinburgh	(B)	904kms
Carlisle	(C)	744kms
Newcastle	(D)	771kms
York	(E)	654kms
Leeds	(F)	633kms
Hull	(G)	662kms
Swansea	(H)	426kms
Holyhead	(J)	692kms
Liverpool	(K)	587kms
Manchester	(L)	568kms
Sheffield	(M)	586kms
Nottingham	(N)	524kms
Cambridge	(O)	577kms
Birmingham	(P)	438kms
Cardiff	(Q)	353kms
Bristol	(R)	310kms
London	(S)	496kms
Dover	(T)	571kms
Brighton	(U)	459kms
Portsmouth	(V)	384kms
Southampton	(W)	352kms
Ipswich	(X)	600kms
Exeter	(Y)	176kms

RIVER TAMAR

It's most likely you crossed into Cornwall over the River Tamar.

THE CHOUGH

The bird on the top of the shield coat of arms is called a Chough.

Sadly it's extinct in the wild in Cornwall, however, Paradise Park near St Ives is breeding these birds to hopefully one day be able to release them back into the area.

CORNWALL'S FLAG

Cornwall's flag is the flag of St Piran the patron saint of miners

Cornwall has its own anthem called The Song of the Western Man

Cornish is a Celtic language which is over 1,000 years old.

3

CARING FOR CORNWALL

LOOKING AFTER THE FUTURE

LEAVE THE CAR BEHIND

By having so many cars on the road we are polluting the air with fumes from engines.

So why not see how many times you can go out without using the car?

WALKING & CYCLING

Walking & Cycling are the best possible ways to really get the most out of your holiday and what's more you're not adding to pollution!

COASTAL PATH

The Coastal Path that runs nearly right the way round Cornwall is quite spectacular.

It can lead you to beautiful beaches, secret coves, Iron Age hill forts and all sorts of other adventures that you would miss if you were travelling on the road.

You can join it almost anywhere in Cornwall by simply walking to your nearest coastal point.

For more details contact the SW Coast Path Association
T: 01752 896237

CYCLING THE CORNISH WAY

There are 6 cycle trails that cover over 280 kilometres through great countryside mostly on small country roads.

Cars are not allowed on the trail from Padstow to Bodmin and the longer trail continuing to Poley Bridge. This makes them extra safe paths for you to cycle on.

Or you could cycle the Coast to Coast Trail from Portreath to Devoran to discover all about Cornish tin mining (see page 26)

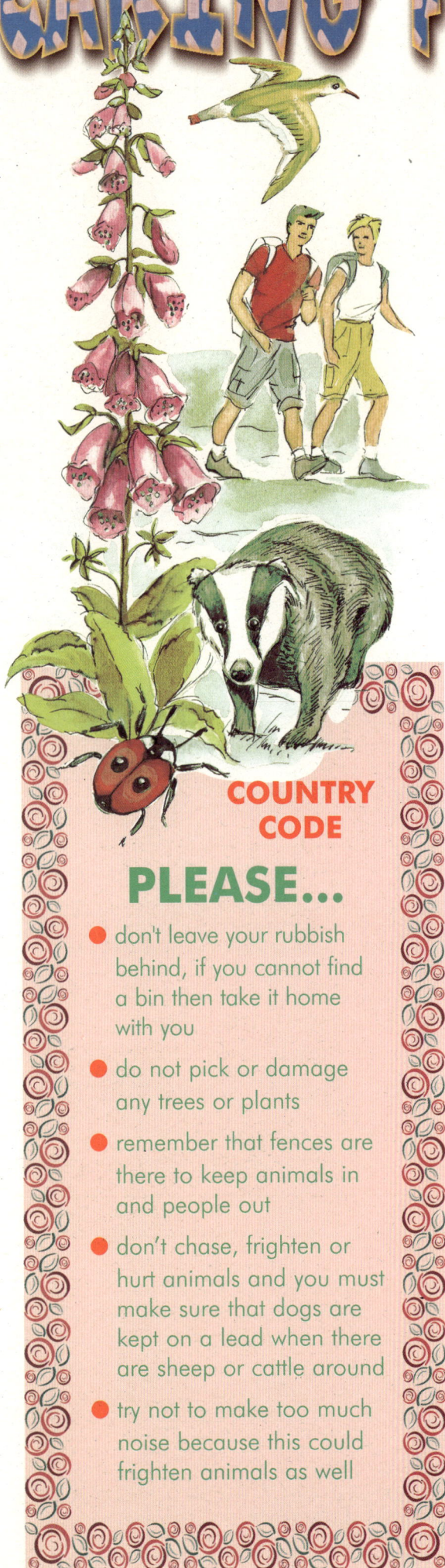

The Cornish Way

COUNTRY CODE

PLEASE...

- don't leave your rubbish behind, if you cannot find a bin then take it home with you

- do not pick or damage any trees or plants

- remember that fences are there to keep animals in and people out

- don't chase, frighten or hurt animals and you must make sure that dogs are kept on a lead when there are sheep or cattle around

- try not to make too much noise because this could frighten animals as well

4

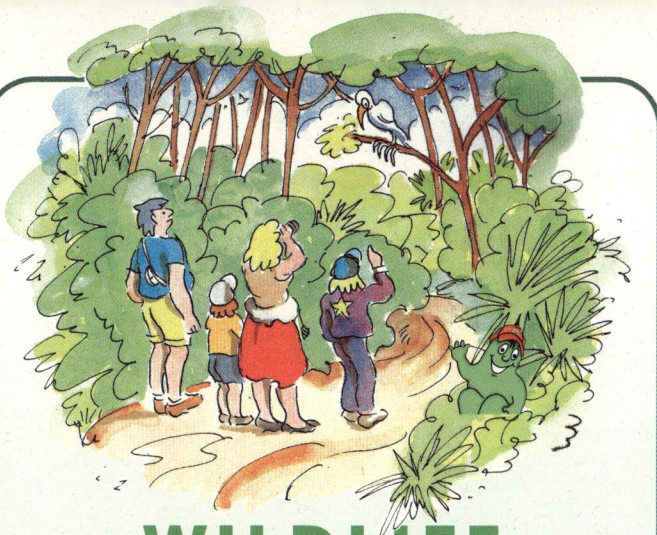

WILDLIFE

Being a careful, caring, curious green detective

It's lots of fun exploring wildlife but there are some very important things you need to remember to become a really good 'green detective'.

Many animals are coloured to blend in with their surroundings so you should try doing the same. Wearing bright coloured clothes could scare the animals away.

Ssssh! Remember some animals have very good hearing so walk slowly and quietly and keep your voice to a whisper. Find somewhere safe to sit and stay as still as you can.

Try shutting your eyes and listening your ears will very often hear things that your eyes can't see.

Be careful but curious. Just by gently lifting up a stone or leaf you will probably discover wrigglie-wiggilies.

But please remember that you are peeking into someone's home so put it back gently the way you found it.

 **1** ☐
 **2** ☐
 **3** ☐

Here's an example of how to score your points

HOW GREEN HAVE YOU BEEN?

Keep a record of the different ways you travelled whilst on your holiday.

DAY	WALKING	CYCLING	BUS	CAR
SATURDAY				
SUNDAY				
MONDAY				
TUESDAY				
WEDNESDAY				
THURSDAY				
FRIDAY				
SATURDAY				
SUNDAY				
MONDAY				
TUESDAY				
WEDNESDAY				
THURSDAY				
FRIDAY				
TOTAL				

CATCH THE BUS

There's a really good network of buses throughout Cornwall and you can get information on them from any of the local tourist centres. (See back page)

How about catching a bus and setting off on a family magical mystery tour?

COLLECTING POINTS

As you explore Cornwall, if you see a flower, bird or sea creature that's in this book then tick the empty box and give yourself the points in the box next to the picture.

For example if the box is blue that means you get one point, yellow you get two points and for a red box you get three points.

At the end of your holiday you can count up your score and fill it in to see just how good a 'green detective' you've been.

A LONG TIME AGO

The Land's End Peninsula is a really exciting place where you can discover how people lived thousands of years ago.

You will come across many mysterious stone monuments, Iron Age villages, burial chambers, secret hideaways, ancient castles and much, much more. So why not become an amateur **archaeologist** on your holiday and find out as much as you can about the history of Land's End?

Men-An-Tol near Morvah

It's thought these three stones might have had something to do with the stars. The doughnut shaped stone is famous for being used to make people feel better.

Children who were not feeling well had to take all their clothes off and go through the hole three times... you would have thought that it would make them feel worse!

FLINT TOOLS

Being able to make simple tools meant ancient people could change the places they lived in.

A flint axe could chop down a tree to clear the land for crops or used as a tool to build a shelter to live in.

Today we call this deforestation and it can affect the wildlife and the environment.

The shape of the tool or weapon was made by hitting flintstone with a harder stone. This is called knapping.

Lanyon Quoit

LANYON QUOIT

Quoits are great stone burial chambers with three or more upright stones that support a massive stone slab called a Capstone. They were often used to bury more than one person.

Archaeologists have often found that the bodies were carefully laid with their heads to the South, men facing East and women facing West. Some people think this was so the corpse could see the sun, the men in the morning the women in the evening.

There are several Quoits in Cornwall. One of the most interesting is Lanyon Quoit near Land's End between Madron and Morvah.

CAN YOU FIND THIS OTHER WELL KNOWN QUOIT? IT'S NEAR BODMIN MOOR

In 8bc Cornwall was named **BELERION** which meant the Shining Land. It was the first place in the British Isles to be given a name.

In 100BC people were farming in the village of Chysauster.

In 1387 a Cornish man called John Trevisa wrote the first book to be printed on English paper.

In 1588 The Spanish Armada was first seen off the coast of Cornwall.

In 1596 one of the first ever loo's was put into Arwenack Manor in Falmouth.

FOGOU SECRET HIDEAWAY?

Fogou is the Cornish word for cave. They are hidden underground passages that have a roof of massive stone.

No one knows for sure what they were used for. If you visit the **Carn Euny Fogou** near Land's End see if you can think of a reason for this mysterious chamber.

Write down in your journal what you think it might have been used for.

CHYSAUSTER
Iron Age Village

You can visit the stone remains of this Iron Age Village and see the courtyards and doorways formed by walls which are still about 1.5 metres high.

The village was lived in from about 100bc to 300ad. When you're exploring the stone walled houses try and imagine what life was like all those years ago.

How do you think they dressed? Do you think that children played with toys like they do know? What animals do you think they kept?

Chysauster, from Treen B3306 St Ives road to Badgers Cross

Artist impression of Chysauster

A legend is a story passed on through the years.

Sacred means something is special for a religious reason.

STONE CIRCLES

You will see stone circles all over Cornwall. It's thought their real purpose was probably as a religious meeting place. Many legends are told about these mysterious places.

At Boleigh near Lands End, the Merry Maidens are a group of 17 stones in a large circle.

Legend tells that these stones were once 17 young girls on their way to church on Sunday. When they heard pipers playing they started to dance. It was a church day so this was very naughty and the story is a thunderbolt turned the girls and the 2 pipers to stone to punish them.

Ancient Road Signs?

There are many of stone crosses and standing stones in Cornwall. Some were used to show the way to **sacred** places but over the years most have been moved.

When you spot one try drawing it on your map of Cornwall.

In 1689 the first mail was sent from Falmouth to Spain

In 1801 Richard Trevithick's Puffing Devil was the first steam engine to carry passengers

In 1815 Sir Humphry Davy invented the Davy Lamp (see page 26)

In 1899 Marconi sent the first radio signals from Poldhu in Cornwall to Canada (see page 39)

In the year 2001 the Eden Project was opened in Cornwall (see page 22)

SAND SEA AND WAVES

EXPLORING THE SEA SHORE

Cornwall has one of the most beautiful coastlines in the world. But as you know some grown-ups seem to think that a day at the beach means a day of lying around in the sun having an occasional dip in the water.

Not only can this be bad for your skin but it can also be very boring and there are far more exciting things to do like: exploring, fishing around in rock pools, watching out for seals, dolphins, basking sharks… even whales and lots more.

Never go in the water or walk along the beach without an adult knowing where you are.

Sea Holly

`1` ☐

FRIENDLY ROOTS!

When you are walking, playing or just picnicking in the sand dunes remember that you are in a very special environment.

The grasses and plants around you may seem prickly or spikey but it's these plants that are holding the dunes together.

Their deep roots make sure that when it's windy the sand is kept together. One plant that is very good at this is Marram Grass.

Marram Grass

`1` ☑

Sea Bindweed

`1` ☐

POLZEATH

F TREVONE AND
G HARLYN BAYS

ROCK

PORTHCOTHAN

NEWQUAY
Watergate
Fistral ❶
Great Western

MAWGAN PORTH

NEWQUAY

PERRINPORTH

GOOD BEACHES AND CLEAN WATER

Cornwall's coast is a treasure trove of beaches and coves. A lot of the fun comes from exploring the coastline and suddenly coming across a beautiful expanse of sand or inlet with exciting rock pools.

To help guide you the dolphin on the map shows where you will find beaches where the water has been tested to make sure it's clean.

PORTREATH

GODREVY TOWANS

CARBIS BAY ▲

HAYLE TOWANS

MOUNTS BAY

PRAA SANDS
A

SENNEN ▲

PORTHCURNO

FALMOUTH
B

FALMOUTH
Gyllyngvase **D**
Swanpool
Maenporth

C

Remember that the sea can pull you out to deep waters so don't use rubber rings or air beds if an adult isn't with you.

KENNARK SANDS
E

Best rock pools:

- **A** Prussia Cove
- **B** Castle Beach
- **C** Bream Cove
- **D** Gyllingvase
- **E** Kennack Sands
- **F** Treyarnon
- **G** Contantine Bay
- **H** Polzeath
- **I** Fistral
- **J** Widemouth Bay
- **K** Porthpean
- **L** Portreath
- **M** Portwrinkle

▲ Other Beaches

■ Marine Centre

BUDE
Crooklets
Summer Lease

WIDEMOUTH SANDS

J

Crustaceans are animals like crabs and lobsters that have hard shells.

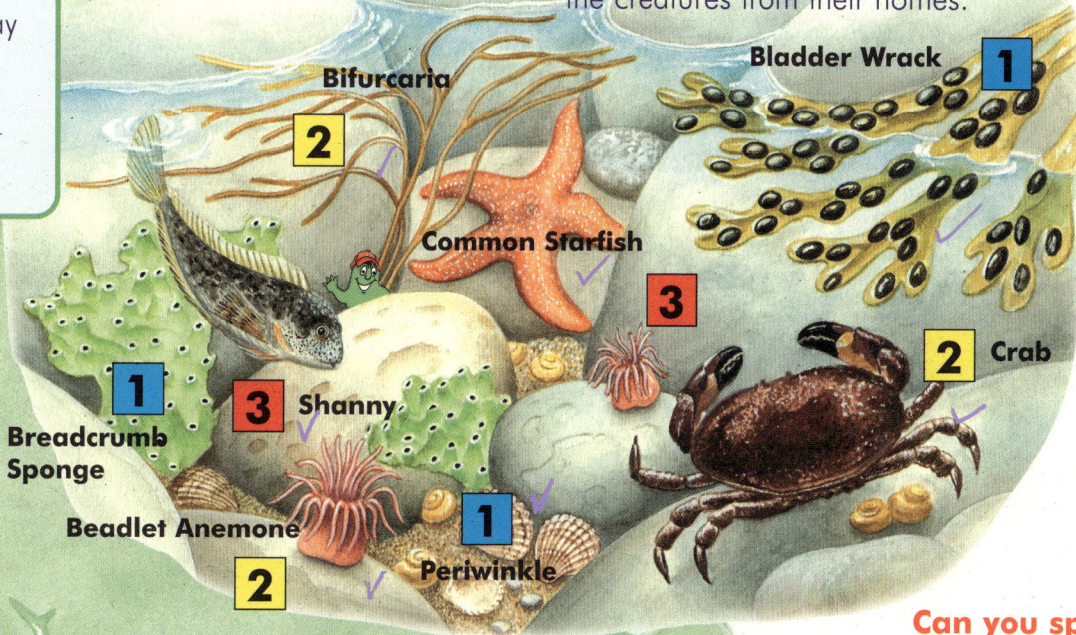

Bifurcaria

2

Common Starfish

Bladder Wrack

1

3

2 Crab

Breadcrumb Sponge

1

3 Shanny

Beadlet Anemone

2

Periwinkle

1

▲ **PAR SANDS**

K

PORTHPEAN

▲ **LOOE**
■

M

When you find any of these creatures or plants, add the number shown in the box to your score.

CAWSANDS AND KINGSANDS

GORREN HAVEN VAULT

TAKE CARE OF THE WILDLIFE

Rock pools are very important to the environment.

They are a home to many animals and lots of fish and **crustaceans** use them as nurseries for their babies.

They are shelter from stormy seas and provide food for other animals and birds.

So have fun discovering and exploring but please don't drop litter or remove any of the creatures from their homes.

Can you spot these shells?

3 ✓ Peppery Furrow Shell

1 ✓ Common Mussel

2 ✓ Painted Topshell

1 ✓ Common Cockle

3 ✓ Dog Whelk

A red flag on a beach means DANGER - NO SWIMMING!

SPOTTERS GUIDE TO
ROCK POOLS

Rock pools are areas by the sea that fill up with seawater twice a day when the tide comes in.

Many of the **crustaceans** that live in them have to be careful not to be swept away when the tide goes out.

Some do this by hiding under rocks or down in the mud and others cling very tightly to the rocks with their suckers.

Take a look inside a rock pool and discover a treasure of little creatures.

9

FISHY BUSINESS

NEWLYN

Newlyn is a busy harbour and home to the second largest fishing fleet in England.

You can walk along the harbour wall and see boats of all sizes.

You can watch the fish being landed, nets repaired and boats being made ready to return to the fishing grounds.

HUER HOUSE

In Newquay overlooking **Fistral Beach** you'll find a tiny whitewashed building called The Huer House.

It was from here that a man, called the Huer, would watch out for the massive shoals of pilchards that used to swarm just off the shore.

His shout of,"Heva" through a large horn to the harbour below would let all the fisherman know that it was time to set sail in their boats.

THE PILCHARD WORKS

At this brilliant museum you can see just how pilchards are processed 'hot of the press'!

You can talk to the people who are working there as well draw your own stencils and find out how people worked and lived in this industry over 100 years ago.

The factory is very concerned about over fishing damaging the environment and tries to make sure all the methods used are environmentally friendly.

The Pilchard Works Newlyn, Penzance.

NATIONAL LOBSTER HATCHERY

At the National Lobster Hatchery they are very serious about caring for the environment. When you go to visit you will be able to explore the world of lobsters and the environment they live in.

Did you know that?
- *Lobsters taste with their feet.*
- *Can be red, blue, white or even have yellow spots.*
- *Have three stomachs.*
- *Can live to be 100 years old.*

The National Lobster Hatchery, South Quay, Padstow.

BLUE REEF AQUARIUM

Blue Reef Aquarium brings the magic of the undersea world alive with over 30 living displays and feeding demonstrations.

There's a walk through an underwater tunnel so you can see coral reefs and sharks close up and open-top tanks where you can actually touch the Ray Fish. You'll find the aquarium on the **Towan Promenade, Newquay.**

At **Mevagissey Sealife Aquarium** you will see different types of local sealife. The money the Aquarium makes from visitors is used to clean up the harbour.

Puffin
3 ☐

COASTAL BIRDS

Cornwall is a wonderful place to see birds that make their home on or near cliffs.

Some live here all the time and others visit at certain times of year, a bit like having a holiday.

Be very careful not to disturb any of them as they are easily frightened and **never go near the edge of cliffs or anywhere else that might be dangerous.**

Shag
2 ✓

Great Black Backed Gull
1 ✓

Razorbill
3 ✓

Herring Gull
1 ✓

Black Head Gull
1 ✓

Cormorant
1 ✓

Fulmer
3 ✓

Guillemot
3 ✓

Camel Estuary

Saltash Estuary

Fal Estuary

Hayle Estuary

Estuary Birds

Birds that live at an estuary are called waders.
The **Camel Estuary** is a really good place to spot waders and so are the **Hayle**, **Fal** and **Saltash Estuaries.**

Turnstone
2 ✓

Lapwing
3 ☐

Little Egret
2 ☐

Rock Pipit
3 ✓

Grey Heron
1 ✓

Oyster Catcher
1 ✓

Red Shank
3 ✓

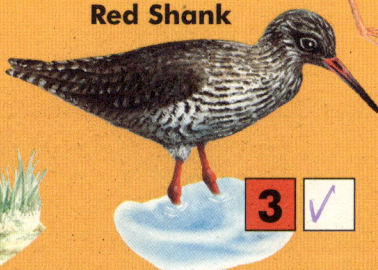

Shelduck
1 ☐

Curlew
2 ☐

11

LIFEBOATS TO THE

Cornwall has the longest and one the most dangerous coastlines of any county in England, so that means it needs to have the largest number of lifeboat stations.

Most of the crew on a lifeboat are volunteers. They have to wear a lot of protective clothing to stop them from becoming cold and wet.

Nowadays lifeboat crew carry pagers to let them know when they are needed for a rescue but years ago a 'maroons' rocket would be let off with an enormous BANG! to let the crew know that their help was needed.

RNLI stands for Royal National Lifeboat Institution

47ft. Tyne Class Lifeboat

HELICOPTER RESCUE

In very special cases the local coastguard will call for extra help from the specially trained helicopter crews from RNSA Culdrose.

They work with the lifeboat men to lift sailors from sinking ships or rescue people who have got into trouble climbing on the cliffs faces.

GOING TO THE RESCUE

There are several types of lifeboats and different ways of launching them.

In the old days the village people and the crew had to drag the boats down from the beach in order to launch them and then row out to the sinking ship.

One of the busiest lifeboats stations in Cornwall is at Lizard Point and it's well worth a visit.

This picture shows the names of the different parts on the Lizard Lifeboat.

1 Engine, 2 Anchor, 3 Watertight Door, 4 Propeller, 5 erial, 6 Navigation Lights, 7 Radar, 8 Steering Wheel, 9 Stretcher, 10 Breeches Buoy, 11 Drogue, 12 Bollard, 14 Coxswain's Seat, 15 Toilet, 16 Searchlight, 17 Loud Hailer, 18 Seat Belts, 19 Radio, 20 Binoculars, 21 Veering Line, 22 First Aid Kit, 23 Fire Extinguisher, 24 Mouth to Mouth Resusitator, 25 Battery, 26 Blue Flashing Light, 28 Haul-up Cleat, 29 Sternlight, 30 Fend-off, 31 Rubber Fendering, 32 Stanchion, 33 Fair Leads, 34 Non-slip Deck Paint, 35 Life Line, 36 Chart & Magnifier

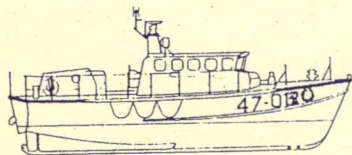

RESCUE

SUPPORTING THE CREWS

St Ives Lifeboat

There are 14 lifeboat stations in Cornwall including the one on the Isles of Scilly.

They often have open days to help raise money for the equipment they need.

There you'll find out about the RNLI and you can even go out on a boat trip.

What's more you'll be supporting a very important service that saves many lives every year.

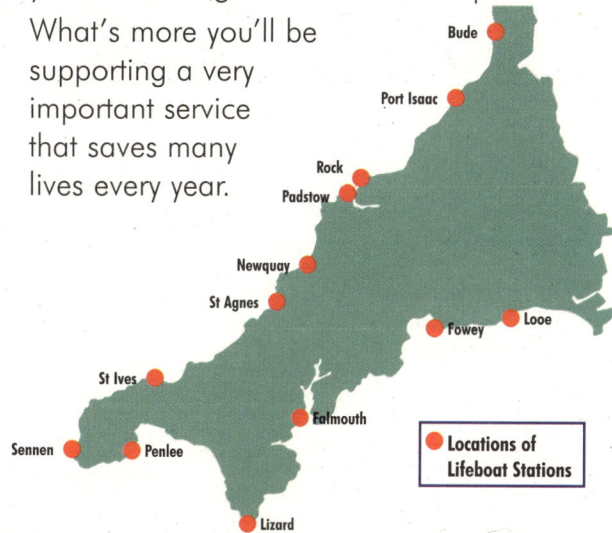

Bude
Port Isaac
Rock
Padstow
Newquay
St Agnes
Fowey
Looe
St Ives
Sennen
Penlee
Falmouth
Lizard

● Locations of Lifeboat Stations

INSHORE LIFEBOATS

Inshore Lifeboats are small, inflatable boats which are just right for helping people who are in trouble close to the seashore. They can be launched quickly and are very fast.

The oldest lifeboat station is at Penlee where there was a horrible tragedy in 1981 when the boat went out on a rescue mission and her crew were all drowned.

DISCOVERING LIGHTHOUSES

Coastal waters can be very dangerous because of rocks that cannot be seen just below the water and also because of the tides.

Penlee Lighthouse

Lighthouses send out a bright beam of light to warn sailors of rocks. Each lighthouse has its own special interval when their light flashes so sailors can recognise the lighthouse and find their position at sea.

Penlee lighthouse is a good example of a working lighthouse and is open to the public.

NATIONAL LIGHTHOUSE CENTRE

Trinity House Centre in Penzance, has probably the largest collection of lighthouse equipment in the world.

There are different **buoys** painted in their special colours. You don't realise how big they are when you have only seen them from a distance, partly submerged.

You will see a full size replica of a lighthouse room, the giant optics they use and enjoy a show which tells the history of the lighthouse.

Buoys are floating markers. They indicate either safe channel's or where there are dangers to avoid.

THE LIZARD LIGHTHOUSE

The first guiding light here was built in 1619 by Sir John Killigrew. He thought he could get passing ships to pay him for keeping them off the rocks. Because so many ships went by without paying, he had to abandon his scheme.

Over the years different types of lighting were used until 1903 when a single 12 million candlepower beam was installed and today it is still one of the most powerful lights in the world.

A WALK IN THE COUNTRY

A BUSY HIGHWAY FOR THE WILDLIFE

Hedgerows are like a corridor for wildlife to travel safely from one place to another.

Small mammals like voles and many birds use hedges to protect them from predators like owls. These mammals also feed on the plants and seeds in the hedgerow.

Butterflies feed on the nectar of the different flowers that grow around hedgerows.

TURF HEDGE

CORNISH HEDGE

SLATE HEDGE

DIFFERENT TYPES OF CORNISH HEDGEROWS

A **Turf Hedge** has earth in the centre with a layer of matted earth made from plant and grass roots on the outside.

A **Cornish Hedge** is a cross between a stone wall and an earth bank they can be seen all over Cornwall.

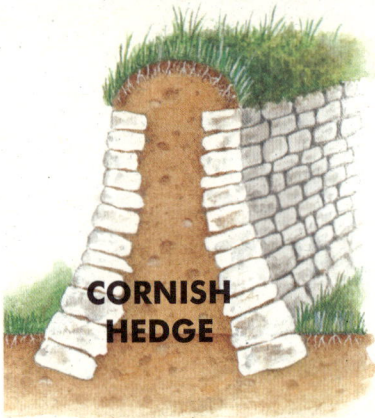

Slate Hedges are mostly found in North Cornwall and are known as Kersey Way Hedges.

Stone Hedges are found mainly on high ground and are full of wild flowers.

CUTTING DOWN THE HEDGEROWS

When hedgerows are cut down lots of plants and animals lose their homes and food supply which leads to many of them either dying out or moving away.

This is just another way that humans can damage the environment.

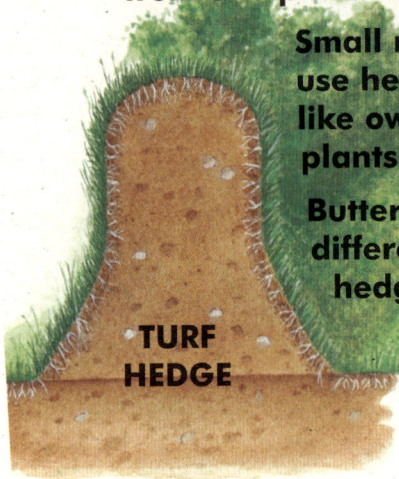

DID YOU KNOW?

The age of a hedgerow can be worked out by counting the number of different types of trees and green perennial shrubs in a 27 metre stretch?

Each type represents one century, that's one hundred years.

The pathway that leads from Lizard Town to Kynance Cove is actually on top of a Cornish Hedge.

Some of the hedgerows in Cornwall date back to the Bronze Age.

There are 150-250 flower species that grow per kilometre in mature hedgerows.

PREDATOR
A living thing that stays alive by eating something else living

PERENNIAL
A plant that produces new growth each year which dies back in the winter

Bodmin Moor

Bodmin Moor is home to masses of wildlife and flowers and some say a few ghosts!

During the Bronze Age a lot of people lived on the Moor and they left behind strange monuments like stones circles that were probably built for religious reasons.

It's here you will find **Brown Willy** which at 420 metres is Cornwall's highest point.

About 1,000 horses and ponies roam free on the Moor. They are an important part of farming life.

The Moor looks very tough but it is a very fragile environment so it's important that we look after it well.

The Cheesewring

is a very strange rock that looks like one flat stone on top of another. It's nearly 7 metres high.

Legend tells that it was made by Giants and Saints having a stone throwing contest, but really it's a natural formation made during the Ice Age.

The Minions

Is a small village high up on Bodmin Moor. At some 300 metres above sea level it's the highest village in Cornwall. There's a heritage centre you can visit to find out about the area.

Bodmin Jail

During the First World War the Doomsday Book, Crown Jewels and other national treasures were kept here for safe keeping and it is now open to the public.

Berrycombe Road, Bodmin

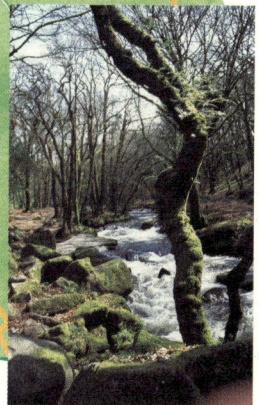

Jamaica Inn

Brown Willy

To Launceston

A30

To Bodmin

Dozemary Pool is said to be where Sir Bedivere threw King Arthur's sword Excalibur to be received by the Lady of the Lake.

Colliford Lake

Goliath Falls

Goliath Falls

THE BEAST OF BODMIN

Since 1983 there have been over 60 reported sightings of a big black cat the size of a leopard on Bodmin Moor.

Not long ago a 14 year old boy found a skull with large fangs on the Moor. The Natural History Museum in London investigated it and decided it was not from an animal commonly found in the English countryside.

So it's still a mystery exactly what the Beast of Bodmin Moor actually is.

Keep your eyes open... you never know you might see it too!!

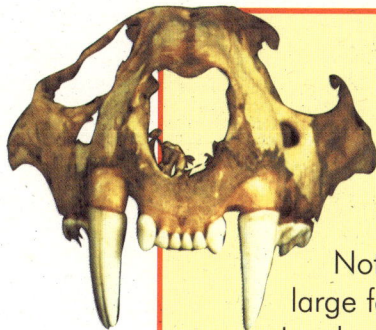

Exploring Cornwall's Rivers & Estuaries

Cornwall has about 526 kilometres of waterways for you to explore and is home to the highest population of Otters in England. If you're lucky you might see some when you're spending time at the river. Otters are very fussy creatures, so if they are living in a certain part of a river that tells us the water there is fairly clean.

LET'S DISCOVER ...

The Tamar River *has a great 48 kilometre Discovery Trail but don't worry, you can walk it in sections! Or you can take a train ride on the Tamar Valley Line.*

The River Camel *has a super path that you can cycle or walk following it all the way from Padstow to Wadebridge seeing lots of different types of estuary birds on your way.*

On **The Fowey River** *you and an adult can hire a canoe and paddle up and down the river from Fowey. You will be accompanied by a safety boat. Take casual clothes like a tracksuit and wear comfortable shoes.*

Fowey Gallery, 17 Passage Street, Fowey

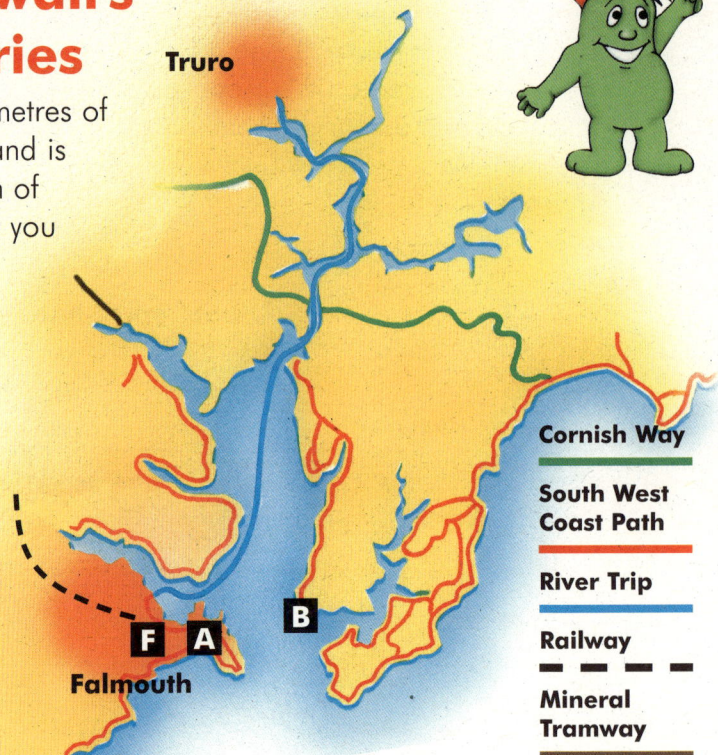

Truro

Falmouth

Cornish Way	
South West Coast Path	
River Trip	
Railway	
Mineral Tramway	

There are many walks along the Helford and Fal River's where you'll discover some lovely old villages. See the wildlife at the *Gweek Seal Sanctuary* or maybe lose yourself in the maze at *Glendurgan Gardens*, or hit the trails at *Trebah Gardens*. You also have an ideal opportunity to explore the twin *castles of Pendennis and St Maws* and the *National Maritime Museum at Falmouth.*

For more information see

A **B**	Pendennis & St Mawes Castle	**page 24**
C **D**	Glendurgan Gardens, Trebah Gardens	**page 23**
E	Gweek Seal Sanctuary	**page 30**
F	Falmouth National Maritime Museum	**page 38**

Red Campion

`1` `✓`

Dog Rose

`1` ` `

Birds Foot Trefoil

`2` ` `

Thrift

`1` ` `

Tormentil

`1` ` `

16

CROSS

Cornish Ferries

There are lots of ferries in Cornwall. Some like the **King Harry Ferry** and **Bodinick Ferry** carry cars as well as passengers across the river.

Trips Along the Fal

From Falmouth Pier you can take a river trip to Truro which is the capital of Cornwall. As you get near to the town you will be able to see **Truro Cathedral** which was built in 1880. It took thirty years to build.

WHERE THE RIVER MEETS THE SEA

An **estuary** is where a river meets up with the sea which means that salt water and fresh water mix together.

This makes them very special places for all sorts of wildlife. Estuaries are good places for fish to lay eggs and hatch their babies.

They are ideal spots for birds flying long distances to rest and eat, a bit like we do in motorway service stations!

Around the edges of estuaries there will often be marshes and wetlands. These act like a filter by cleaning the water before it reaches the estuary.

The **Padstow Estuary** is one of the only places in England where you can see all the features that make up an estuary.

Sea Stock 3 ☐

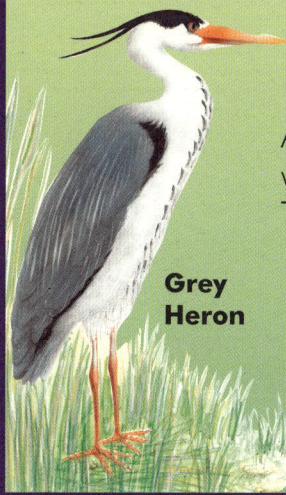

Grey Heron

Wild Flowers

It's great fun to spot and name wild flowers. They grow everywhere in Cornwall from hedgerows to moorland, riverside to seaside.

If you are new to wild flower spotting it's a good idea to buy a guide that will help you to identify the different flowers you see.

To start you off here are some flowers you can find growing in Cornwall. When you spot one tick the box next to it and collect your points.

1 ☑

Honeysuckle

Rock Spurrey

2 ☐

Sea Campion

1 ☐

Scarlet Pimpernel

1 ☐

Tree Mallow

2 ☐

Foxglove

2 ☑

BIRDS AND BUTTERFLIES

Greater Spotted Woodpecker

3 ✓

Bird Watching

Though it would be great to have a pair of binoculars you don't have to have them to enjoy bird watching.

What you do need to do is keep as quiet and still as possible because birds are very sensitive to sound and movement and will fly away quickly if disturbed.

Why not make a note in your journal of the birds you see? That way you can look them up in a book or on the web when you get home to find out what they were.

If you have a camera try taking a few photos to help you remember what the bird looked like.

Green Woodpecker

3 ✓

Raven

1 ✓

Robin

1 ✓

Swift

1 ✓

Black Cap

3

Cuckoo

3 ✓

2 ✓

Chaffinch

1 ✓ **Magpie**

Jay

2 ✓

2

Grey Wagtail

Birds of prey

There are over 200 different kinds of Birds of Prey in the world.

They have sharp eyesight, strong legs with sharp claws.

Because of pesticides used in farming poisoning their food they are not that common.

Another name for a bird of prey is a Raptor. Watch out for these birds as you walk in the countryside (see page 32).

Buzzard

3 ✓

Sparrow Hawk

3

Kestrel

3 ✓

Butterflies have four different stages to their life.

The Comma Butterfly.

First of all the adult butterfly lays an egg the size of a pin head.

1

The egg hatches into a caterpillar (sometimes called larva). The caterpillar eats a lot of food and grows very quickly.

2

Then the caterpillar forms a chrysalis or pupa and hangs upside down from a twig or a leaf.

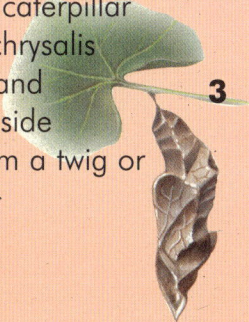

3

Inside the chrysalis the caterpillar changes into a butterfly, and out comes...

4

The Comma `1` ✓

BUTTERFLY CONSERVATION

Because we stopped being careful with our countryside butterflies have started to become less in number.

For example if we put up buildings where there used to be meadows we destroy the plants that the butterflies feed on.

When you get home how about planting a little butterfly garden? You can get special seeds which will grow into plants that butterflies love. It does not have to be a very big piece of garden - you could even use a window box.

Did you know 5 butterflies are now extinct in the UK?

`1` ✓ **Painted Lady**

Peacock `1`

Small Pearl Bordered Fritillary `3`

`1` **Gatekeeper**

`2` ✓ **Common Blue**

Wall `2`

`1` ✓ **Speckled Wood**

`2` **Marbled White**

CREATE YOUR OWN BUTTERFLY

Butterflies only live for a short time. They cannot eat, they can only drink. If there are butterflies around that's a good sign that the environment is healthy.

CUSTOMS, LEGENDS & FESTIVALS

THE OBBY OSS, FESTIVAL Padstow.

The fearsome looking Obby Oss appears in the streets of Padstow on the 1st of May.

It dances wildly through the town chased by someone called a teaser. People have been dressing up this way once every year for centuries to celebrate the first day of summer.

The streets are decorated with beautiful spring flowers and the town's people of Padstow come out to follow the procession. The children dress up like the Obby Oss and parade through the streets having lots of fun.

A custom is a usual way of behaving or doing something

The Golowan Festival

This festival in **Penzance** is held over 10 days in June and celebrates the Feast of St John. Every day is packed full of fabulous things to see and activities to take part in.

Mazey Day is terrific fun with the local school children and teachers dressing up in costumes they have made and parading through the streets to the music of a brass band.

HELSTONS FURRY DANCE is one of oldest **customs** in England. It celebrates the beginning of Spring. The children wear white, the ladies dress up in their finest clothes and gentlemen wear top hats and tails.

They dance to brass bands that lead them through the streets. The Furry Dance takes place at the beginning of May.

THE DEVIL PROOF HOUSES OF VERYAN

In this village you will find 5 circular houses built by a local vicar. He was really worried that the Devil would try to get into the village, so he had these round houses built, each with a cross on the roof, so the Devil would have no corners to hide in to lay in wait for the owners.

Where **Tintagel Castle** stands today there used to be a monastery, legend tells that it was here that King Arthur was born to Queen Igerna way back in the 1st Century.

There are very many stories about King Arthur, his wife Guinevere, his friend Sir Lancelot and the Knights of the Round Table but as they are from the 12th century it's very difficult to know what was true and what has been made up.

However, the stories themselves are so wonderful and the area in Cornwall where the legends are based is so beautiful and magical, that it's well worth exploring.

King Arthur tried to build a fair society where everyone could live in peace. Unfortunately this was not possible because his nephew Mordred wanted not only Arthur's kingdom but also his wife Guinevere!

King Arthur died in the battle he fought with Mordred and his friend Sir Bedivere threw the sword Excalibur into **Dozebury Pool** to be received by the Lady of the Lake.

If you visit **The Arthurian Centre** in Camelford you'll be able to see the stone said to mark the spot where he died at **Slaughton Bridge** (see page 36).

The most famous story tells of Arthur being the only person who could pull the sword Excalibur out of a stone.

The lady of the lake holds the sword thrown by Sir Bedivere.

MERMAID OF ZENNOR

In the **church at Zennor** look for a special bench with a carving of a mermaid on the end. Legend says she had fallen in love with the voice of the squires son who sung in the choir and she came out of the sea and took him back with her to the bottom of the ocean.

Some people think they can sometimes hear his singing even now.

Cornish Piskies

In the olden days the people of Cornwall believed they shared their land with fairies and piskies.

The Piskies wore little red caps, white waistcoats, green stockings, brown coats and very shiny shoes, buckled with diamond dew drops.

Sometimes they got up to mischief but they could be very helpful to older people who could find their cleaning and gardening done as if by magic.

Colour in the Piskie and give him a name.

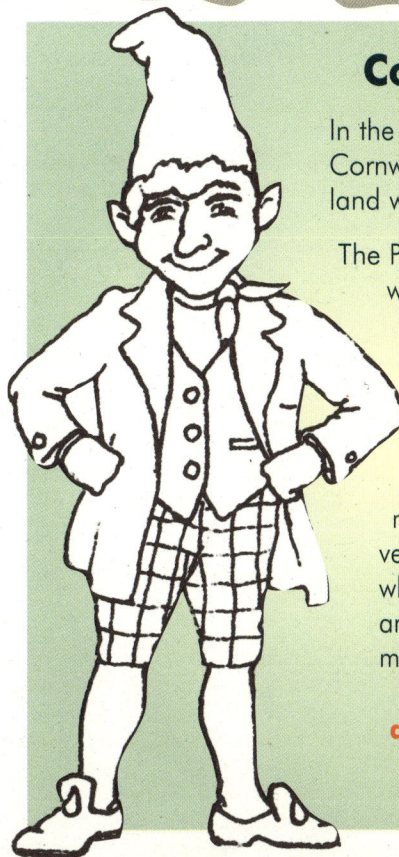

....

EDEN PROJECT

A WALK IN THE RAIN FOREST IN THE WORLD'S LARGEST GREENHOUSE

Here you can learn about plants the world over and how we can look after them and our planet. You can go on adventure trails through the Rain Forest and see, smell and touch plants that supply our food and drink, are used to make clothes to keep us warm and supply the material to build our homes.

You will find out where things you use everyday (like toothpaste hopefully!) come from and while you are exploring you will be able to hear and see the spectacular waterfall that roars down from the massive roof into the forest of Amazonia.

This vibrating, 5 metre long bumble bee reminds you of the importance of pollination. Pollination is how plants multiply themselves and bumble bees are just one of the insects that help them to do this.

Learning how to weave wicker

There are lots of opportunities to take part in all sorts of activities that are especially planned for children.

The Outdoor Landscape is a collection of plants and flowers from all over the world that constantly changes depending on the season.

The Eden Project is the size of 35 football pitches and 50 metres deep. As huge as it is it's completely hidden from view until you go through the visitors centre.

The Humid Tropic and the Warm Temperate Biomes are host to plants, fruits and flowers from all over the world.

Humid Tropics Biome
05
02
03
01
04
Early Exit
Café
The Link
Easy access toilets
Toilets
10
7
Restaurant
Biome Entrance
Takeaway
Warm Temperate Biome
01
02
03
05
04
13
The West Side
20
05
Land Train
Takeaway
21
Eden Arena
Outdoor Landscape
The Zigzag
Education Centre
Toilets
Easy access toilets
27
Takeaway
Eden Village
Viewpoint
22
Viewpoint
Viewpoint
Land Train
Restaurant
Information
Tickets
Café
Toilets
Easy access toilets
Shop
Plant sales
Visitor Centre

The environment is the surroundings that people, animals, plants and organisms are living in.

Quiz

Give yourself a point for each question you get right and add it to your 'green detectives' score at the back of the book.

1 Which plant has the biggest leaf in the HT Biome?

2 Which plant is the hungriest?

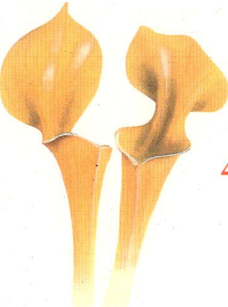

3 Which is the biggest seed?

4 Which is the fastest moving plant?

5 Which are the smallest seeds?

6 What is the most expensive spice?

7 Which are the oldest trees?

8 Which is the worst smelling plant?

9 What is the hottest chilli pepper?

10 Which is the rarest plant?

Answers

Answers 1) Victorian Giant water Lily 2) Pitcher Plant 3) Coco de mer 4) Sensitive plant 5) Orchids 6) saffron 7) Olive trees 8)Dutchman's Pipe 9) 'Birds-eye', 10) Jelly Fish

The **Humid Tropics Biome** is the worlds largest conservatory, 240 metres long,110 metres wide and 50 metres high. Here plants from Malaysia, West Africa and Tropical South America are grown.

The **Warm Temperate Biome** contains plants from South Africa, The Mediterranean and America

GLENDURGAN GARDENS

These gardens are on the shore of the Helston Estuary.

Here you will see masses of wildflowers and exotic trees and plants. There's also a **fabulous laurel maze** that was built in 1833 and the Giant's Stride which looks a bit like a maypole that you can swing on.

Glendurgan Gardens, Mawnan Smith, Falmouth.

TREBAH GARDENS

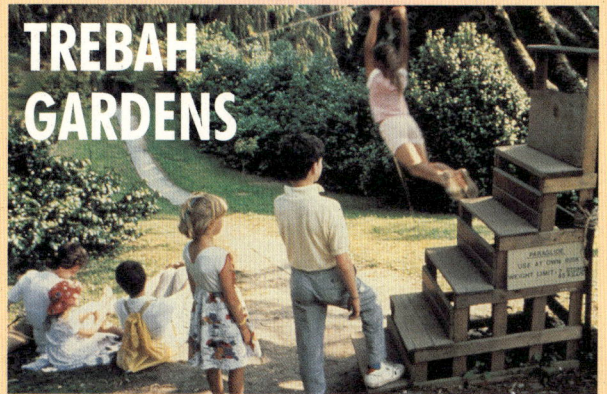

A very special garden with lots of hidden paths and passages just waiting to be investigated.

There's lots to do and see like exploring the Trebah Trail with a map that you can draw the plants and animals on when you find them.

Trebah Gardens, Mawnan Smith near Falmouth.

EDEN BRANCH LINE

The Eden Project have taken a lot of trouble to try and make sure visitors use public transport rather than their own cars.

You can buy a train ticket which includes a bus transfer from the nearest station call 08457 484950 for details.

www.edenproject.com

CORNISH CASTLES

Pendennis Castle

PENDENNIS & ST MAWES CASTLES

When Henry VIII divorced his French wife Catherine of Aragon, France became very angry. So Henry decided he should protect the south coast in case the French decided to attack England.

These twin castles face each other across the mouth of the River Fal and are part of the King's Coastal Defence. Any enemy ship trying to use the river would be caught in the cross-fire from these castles.

The Civil War

In 1646 the garrison of Pendennis Castle bravely refused to surrender to Oliver Cromwell's troops and managed to hold out for six months.

Eventually with only horse and dog meat left to eat, the castle was surrendered.

St Mawes Castle on the other hand had to surrender at once because it had no defences from a land attack. Even so it is regarded as Henry VIII's most perfect coastal defence.

Pendennis Castle is a great place to see the various gun emplacements and tour the secret underground wartime defences.

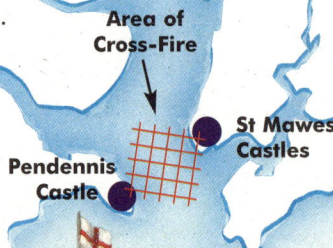

Area of Cross-Fire

St Mawes Castles

Pendennis Castle

St Mawes Castle

Artillery Forts

King Henry's Artillery Forts are specially designed coastal defences. They were round with very thick walls so enemy canonballs would be redirected off the curved surfaces.

They were also built not very high off the ground so it was difficult for enemy ships to get a good shot at them from the sea.

Being round meant that cannons could fire in all directions from the gun platforms.

LAUNCESTON CASTLE

You can't help seeing the remains of this Norman Castle as you enter Launceston because it's built on top of a huge, natural hill that overlooks the town.

Although not much of this ancient stronghold remains it's still worth a visit to see the surrounding countryside and the town from the top of the hill.

Launceston was the chief castle of Richard Earl of Cornwall. From there his men could control the river crossing in and out of the county.

The town itself was the only walled town in Cornwall.

Launceston Castle

St Michaels Mount

ST MICHAELS MOUNT

St Michaels Mount becomes an island when the tide comes in so sometimes you can walk over to it across the causeway and at other times you must take the ferry.

If you visit the chapel watch out for the dungeon where the skeleton of a man almost 2.13 metres tall was found. He was thought to have been the tallest person ever recorded in Britain.

RESTORMEL CASTLE

Restormel Castle was built over 900 years ago which makes it one of the oldest motte-and-bailey castles in Cornwall.

You can still make out the ruins of the Keep, main gate and Great Hall and even the kitchens and private rooms.

The castles defences were very impressive with the walls built behind a 17 metre moat. Charles II's army drove out the parliamentarian garrison from here during the Civil War in 1644 which was the only time that this castle saw any action.

The castle is situated near Lostwithiel.

Tintagel Castle

Tinatagel Castle was built in 1145 and the remains of the building are surrounded by many myths and legends and of stories about King Arthur and the Wizard Merlin and his magic spells and conjuring.

The castle is built on the very edge of the cliffs and over the centuries the sea has worn away at the land so the castle is now in two parts, one being on the mainland and one being on the peninsula.

If you want to learn more about King Arthur, Merlin and The Round Table then visit the **Tintagel Visitors Centre** (see page 36).

Motte and Bailey's

The very first Motte and Bailey Castles were made of wood. The Castle Keep was built on top of a steep mound called a Motte. Which made it the safest part within the castle defences. Connected to the Castle Keep was an area called a Bailey. When an attack began the villagers would take themselves and their animals, into the bailey and pull-up the gate. The entire area was surrounded by a moat or ditch but they did not always have water in them. Later, stone replaced the wooden castles.

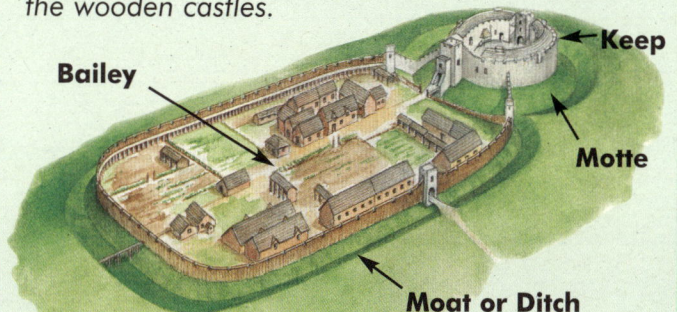

Bailey — Keep — Motte — Moat or Ditch

An artist impression of how Restormel may have looked about 1300 using the Motte and Bailey idea.

25

HOLES IN THE GROUND

"Wherever there's a hole in the ground a Cornishman will be found at the bottom"

Tin mining began in Cornwall during the Bronze Age. Tin is the main ingredient of bronze and the Bronze Age people used it to make weapons and tools.

Tin and copper mines were once Cornwall's biggest industry but they were not making very much money so lots of Cornish miners went to live in other countries that needed the help of people who had a lot of experience in the mining industry.

By 1750 there were thousands of people working in the mines and they were not all grown-ups because children were expected to work as well in those days.

Sir Humphry Davy
(1778-1829)

Working in the mines was a very dangerous business and many men and boys died every year.

The main causes of death were either rock falls or explosions of the gases given off in the mines.

Sir Humphry Davy invented a lamp that warned the miners when gases were present so they could get themselves out of the way of danger.

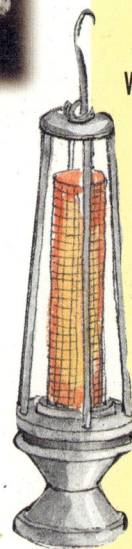

The Mineral Tramway Trail

You can find out a lot about the ancient mining industry when you visit the Camborne and Redruth areas. There's a mineral tramway trail that you can walk or cycle and there are 3 different paths to choose from. The Coast to Coast Trail is 19.5kms long and it runs from Portreath on the North Coast to Devoran, near Falmouth. As you walk or cycle along this trail you will be travelling on the first ever railway track in Cornwall where horse drawn wagons used to pull heavy loads.

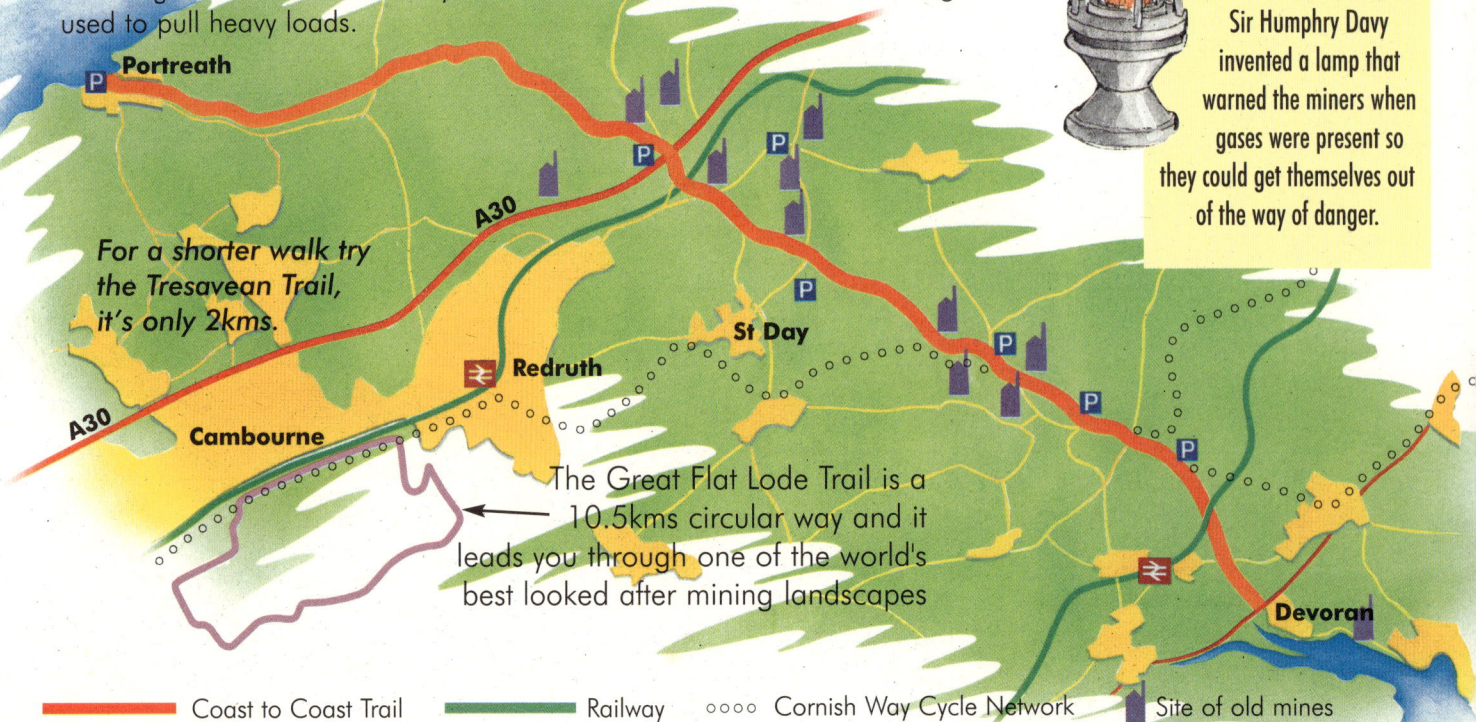

For a shorter walk try the Tresavean Trail, it's only 2kms.

The Great Flat Lode Trail is a 10.5kms circular way and it leads you through one of the world's best looked after mining landscapes

Portreath

A30

A30

Cambourne

Redruth

St Day

Devoran

―――― Coast to Coast Trail   ―――― Railway   ooooo Cornish Way Cycle Network   ■ Site of old mines

UNDERGROUND MINE TOURS

THE POLDARK MINE

No matter what the weather you'll really enjoy exploring this mine museum and imagining what it was like to be a miner in the eighteenth century with just a candle in your hat for light.

You can explore the underground workings and post your letter from the deepest post box in Britain! Then take a walk around the beautiful woodland area.

Poldark Mine, Wendron, Near Helston

GEEVOR TIN MINE

Up until 1990 this mine was still working but now it's open to visitors and you can take a tour with an experienced guide to see just how terrible conditions were for working miners back in the 1800's. The mine workings reach out right under the sea.

Geevor Tin Mine and Heritage Centre Pendeen, Penzance

Find the statues

There are statues of two Cornishmen who are very famous for their inventions. One is in Penzance and the other is in Camborne. When you find them write down their names in your log book and what they are famous for, then give yourself 2 points for each answer on your score card at the back of your book.

Cornwall's Industrial Discovery Centre

If you're interested in engines then you'll have a great time discovering all about them at the centre.

There's also a short film shown on five different screens in an audio visual room that explains Cornwall's working history.

Cornwall's Industrial Discovery Centre, Pool, 2 miles west of Redruth

Wheal Martyn China Clay Heritage Centre

All around you are things that need clay to make them, maybe even the paper you're holding in your hands right now.

When the Works opened in the 1800's many boys of 14 years or younger would go there to work, fetching and carrying tools and making tea. They were called Kettle or Tool Boys and were paid about 6 old pence a day, today that's about 2p.

You will learn the history of the Works and there's a great nature trail with woodland and wetlands, you can also enjoy a commando style adventure.

Wheal Martyn China Clay Heritage Centre, St Austell

DELABOLE SLATE QUARRY

At Delabole State Quarry you can discover Europes largest man made hole in the ground where men have been digging for over 600 years. You can still watch the men splitting the slate and have a guided tour around the site.

Delabole Slate Company, Pengelly, Delabole

A TASTE OF CORNWALL

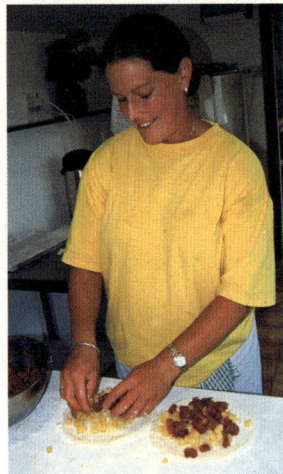

THE CORNISH PASTY

Making a Cornish Pasty at Anne's Pasty Shop

The Cornish Pasty has been a traditional food in Cornwall for centuries. They were made to be a meal in themselves, for the farmer out in the middle of a field or the miner hundreds of feet underground.

The traditional ingredients of a Cornish Pasty are beef, potatoes, onion and turnip wrapped up inside short crust pastry. You can watch them being made at **Anne's Pasty Shop, in Lizard town.**

True or False?

There's a story that says that the crimping that finishes off the edges of the pasties has a historical meaning.

The miners hands were often covered in arsenic, a very dangerous poison, and the crimping meant they could eat the pasty holding the edge and throw it away when they'd eaten the rest. That way they wouldn't get a really bad tummy ache!

Is a Pasty called an Oggy?

If you've never had Cornish Ice Cream then it's about time you did, it's absolutely delicious.

Most of the places where it is made in Cornwall make sure that only top quality ingredients are used.

At **Roskilly's Farm** you can actually watch the cows being milked and find out how the ice cream is made. Of course you also get to try it too which can't be bad!

Roskilly's Farm Tregellast Barton, near Helston.

THE CORNISH CIDER FARM

Why not visit a working cider farm where you can see over forty varieties of fruit products including jams, honey and chutneys all of which you can taste?

There's a guided tour that takes you through the press house, jam kitchen and cider museum. You can also go on a tractor ride through the orchards.

There's even a pottery where you can have a go at 'throwing' your own pot.

The Cornish Cyder Farm, Penhallow, Truro.

Mead and cider are Cornwall's most famous drinks they both taste sweet and fruity and they are very boozy!

Traditional mead is made from honey and traditonal cider from farmhouse apples called bittersharps and bittersweets. To make the cider the apples are squashed and left in barrels.

STAR GAZEY PIE

Star Gazey Pie is quite a wonder to behold! It's made with cleaned, boned and de-headed pilchards that are rubbed with salt and pepper, laid in a pie dish and then covered with thick milk and a pastry crust.

The pilchards heads stick out from the top of the pie with their tails tucked under the rim of the pastry.

Whats odd about this pie?

Answer:
There are 6 fish heads but seven tails

MOUSEHOLE STORY

The story of how this pie came to be made goes back many years when a terrible storm had cut off the village of Mousehole and the population were starving.

Tom Bawcock a brave fisherman set off through the rough seas to bring back fish so the village people could eat.

Traditionally now the pie is made and eaten on the 23rd December which is known as Tom Bawcock Eve.

Visiting the Local Farmers Markets

Because it is so important to the environment to try and produce food locally, Farmers Markets are held on a regular basis in many Cornish towns and they are great fun to visit.

You'll find stalls selling all sorts of different foods and also local craftwork. Buying things that have been grown or made locally means your helping to reduce traffic on the roads and that means less pollution from the fuel the lorries use.

So when you buy things locally you are:
**Supporting the local economy
Reducing transport costs &
helping to improve the environment
by reducing pollution from fuel.**

Check with your local tourist board for places and times

DID YOU KNOW...

when a glass bottle is thrown away it takes a thousand years to bio-degrade?

A plastic container takes 500 years and a tin can also 500 years.

These are excellent reasons for taking your containers home with you and recycling them don't you think?

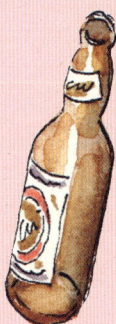

CORNISH CREAM TEAS

Cream teas are a traditional Cornish snack. They are scones with strawberry jam and Cornish clotted cream on top.

There are a great many places where you can dig into this lovely treat. Just watch for the cream tea signs.

THE NATURAL WORLD

All over Cornwall there are many people who work very hard to provide care and shelter for animals who can't look after themselves. The places they work in are often called sanctuaries.

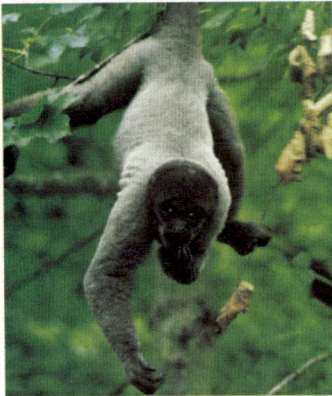

Conservation means to protect and care for

THE WOOLLEY MONKEY SANCTUARY

This Sanctuary first opened to look after Woolley Monkeys who were being kept in small cages in zoos or as pets to let them live as natural a life as possible.

This sanctuary provided such a wonderful home for these monkeys that it became the first place where the Woolley Monkeys ever survived and bred outside of their natural home which is in The Amazon Rainforest in South America.

Monkey Talk

Eeolk! means, "Hello! Where are you?"

Chuckle! means, "I want to play".

Monkey Sanctuary Looe.

NATIONAL SEAL SANCTUARY

Did you know seals can sleep lying on their backs in the water and if a wave rolls over them their nostrils close automatically?

You can find out lots more about seals and see them in safe and happy surroundings at this seal sanctuary.

Around thirty seals are rescued each year and cared for until it's safe for them to return to the sea.

Sometimes a seal won't be able to look after itself in the wild so the sanctuary provides them with a permanent home.

The National Seal Sanctuary, Gweek, near Helston

Tamar Otter Sanctuary

Otters are very sensitive animals so it's important that we take special care of them.

At this sanctuary they not only care for Otters but also have a dormouse **conservation** project plus Deer, Peacocks, Golden Pheasants and Wallabies all being kept safe from harm.

North Petherwin, Launceston

NEWQUAY ZOO

Newquay Zoo is home to many endangered species of animal. The zoo takes great care to ensure that all the animals are happy and healthy.

For example when the lions are fed their meat is hidden in different parts of their enclosure so that they have to 'hunt' around for it - a little bit like they would have to do in the wild.

You can also get close to the worlds smallest monkey, the Pygmy Marmoset and see Roxy the Sloth who had to be hand reared at the zoo.

Newquay Zoo, Trenance Gardens, Newquay

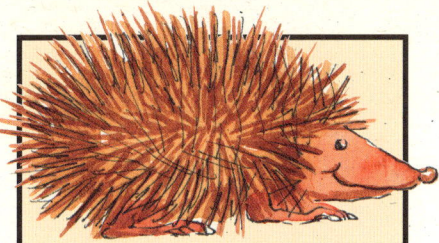

HEDGEHOG HOSPITAL

Newquay Zoo Hospital looks after several hundred injured hedgehogs every year.

Why not go along and meet the patients and find out what you can do to help Britains native wildlife?

Make notes in your journal about all the different animals you see. **They'll be a great way to remind you of your experiences.**

Portreath Bee Centre, near Wadebridge

Have you ever heard the expression, 'busy as a bee'? Well, once you've seen how hard bees work you'll understand where it came from and if you're a Winnie the Pooh fan you can also visit 'Pooh Corner'.

PORFELL ANIMAL LAND

Along with many other animals you will also see Bert the Capybara at Animal Land. Capybara's are the world's largest rodents.

They got their name from the native people of South America which is where they come from. The word capybara means "master of the grass".

You will also be able to learn all about the animals, trees and plants that you see as well as being able to hand feed and pet some of the animals.

Porfell Animal Land Trecangate, Liskeard

TAMAR VALLEY DONKEY PARK
ST ANN'S CHAPEL, GUNNISLAKE

It's very hard to understand how people can be cruel to animals but unfortunately some are. So thank goodness for places like the Donkey Sanctuary.

Here donkeys and ponies are given safe, loving homes and you can go and visit them to see just how happy they are.

BIRD PARKS AND SANCTUARY

PARADISE BIRD PARK

Not only can you see lots of rare and beautiful creatures at Paradise Park but they are also home to the World Parrot Trust.

There's plenty of space for you to play and meet friendly animals, you might even get chosen to help feed the penguins.

There's a 'World Explorer' quiz trail for all visiting children. You fill in the questionnaire as you explore the Park and then you can claim a special badge and have your certificate stamped as a reward.

Paridise Bird Park, Hayle.

Did you know that parrots can live to be over 50 years old?

A bird of prey is a bird that hunts, catches and eats live animals like mice.

MOUSEHOLE BIRD HOSPITAL

Over many years this hospital has had to cope with thousands of birds in need of care and attention. They always aim to help the birds return to the wild but those who are not well enough to leave are looked after for the rest of their lives.

Mousehole Bird Hospital Raginnis Hill, Mousehole, near Penzance.

The Cornish Birds of Prey Centre

Here you can see Hawks, Falcons, Owls, Peregrines and Buzzards. There's a real character called 'Bones' the Vulture and "ET" the Bengalese Eagle Owl who is quite a comedian!

There are regular flying displays where you can see a falcon "stoop" at over 289 kilometres an hour!

But perhaps best of all you actually get to handle and touch the birds which gives you the chance to find out so much more about them.

The Centre is situated on the A39 at Winnards Perch which is between St Columb Major and Wadebridge.

Screech Owl Sanctuary

There are over a hundred owls here and some are hand-tame so you can touch them. The people who work here know all about owls and are more than happy to tell you about them and answer your questions.

At certain times of year you can also see baby owls playing in their nursery.

Screech Owl Sanctuary, Indian Queens, Goss Moor.

PLACES TO GO

FLAMBARDS VILLAGE THEME PARK, HELSTON

You'll have so much fun at Flambards no matter what the weather. They have internationally famous exhibitions, exciting rides, playgrounds, family shows, beautiful gardens plus the recreation of a Victorian village and Britain during the Blitz of the Second World War.

In the Victorian village you can walk along a lamp-lit street with over 50 shops and homes shown exactly like they were in Victorian times.

The Creepy-Crawly Wildlife Show lets you see spider's and snake's close up, maybe you'll even get to hold them!

Gaia Energy Centre

Here you will find out in a really fun way how we can use the wind and water to make light and heat.

By carefully recycling and also using things that would normally get thrown away, we can all help the environment which will cut down on global warming.

There are lots of interactive things for you to have fun with while finding out how to look after our planet.

Gaia Energy Centre, Delabole

LAKESIDE ADVENTURE PARK

At Lakeside they are working very hard to protect and increase a number of wild animals like barn owls and red squirrels.

There's an educational area where you can explore the different ways of making energy using sustainable resources like sun, water and wind power.

Then there's the adventure play grounds, a nature conservation area where you can go into a hide a watch for birds and all sorts of other activities to keep you busy.

Lakeside Adventure Park, Bolventor, Bodmin Moor

GOONHILLY EARTH STATION

Goonhilly Earth Station is the largest satellite earth station in the world. Here you can discover how live television pictures arrive in your living room. You can operate a satellite dish and even turn yourself into 3D computer image!

Plus you get a chance to be really close to the gigantic dishes that send and receive signals to and from space.

There is a cinema which will take you on an exciting journey through time and space all sorts of fascinating things to do and find out about.

Goonhilly Earth Station, near Helston.

33

MORE TO DO...

LAND'S END THEME PARK

At the very tip of England, you will find a wonderful mixture of great things to do and see. There are brilliant nature trails waiting to be explored where you'll see wild flowers and birds living in their natural habitat.

There are lots of fun activities like the Last Labyrinth that takes you down into the depths of Lands End itself for a fabulous multimedia show.

Then there's the Land of Greeb with an animal farm and a cottage kept just as it would have been 200 hundred years ago and lots, lots more to enjoy and do.

TRETHORNE LEISURE FARM

If the weather's not too good you'll still have heaps of fun at this indoor entertainment centre with giant slides and trampolines, there's even a roller blading room.

Around the farm itself there's a wonderful collection of animals you can feed, milk, ride and cuddle, not to forget Arnie and Libby the pot-bellied pigs.

Trethorne Leisure Farm, Kennards House, Near Launceston

Dairyland Farmworld

Believe it or not at Dairyland there's a pretend cow called Clarabelle who looks and feels like the real thing and you can have a go at milking her yourself.

Not only that but at this farmpark there are lots of farm animals and some great rides for you to go on, plus a fabulous nature trail with all kinds of wildlife for you to spot.

Dairyland Farmworld near Newquay

BROCKLANDS ADVENTURE PARK

Not only is there a wonderful adventure park with karts, trampolines and other fun things to do here but also there is a wildlife walk which takes you to a beautiful pond and waterfall.

Information boards all along the route tell you about the wildlife and you can even pick up a questonnaire sheet to fill in as you follow the trail - they also give you a sheet with the answers on in case you get really stuck!

Brocklands Adventure Park, Kilkhampton, Bude.

WORLD IN MINIATURE

Set in 12 acres of gardens, you can explore all sorts of facinating places from around the world. However, the realistic buildings and statues are all in miniature. Buckingham Palace, The Statue of Liberty and the Taj Mahal are just a few interesting minature building in this collection.

Or, if you wish, you can go back in time and walk amongst the pre-historic animals that roamed the earth in the Jurassic period.

World in Miniature, Goonhaven, Nr Perranporth

WATER WORLD

Edgcumbe Avenue, Newquay.

You'll have a great time sliding down the 60m water flume into the tropical fun pool.

When you have had enough fun in the water there's crazy golf, a miniature railway, a boating lake, toboggans and a whole lot more.

Shires Family Adventure Park

As well as terrific rides and slides, including the Raging River Water Coaster, there are cart rides, a working museum, beautiful shire horses, stallions and other animals for you to see and find out about.

Don't miss visiting the Haunted Castle where you might bump into a few skeletons and ghosts and then get a breath of fresh air in the Enchanted Forest and meet the woodland creatures.

Shires Family, Adventure Park, Wadebridge.

HOLYWELL BAY FUN PARK

You'll have an excellent time playing crazy golf and losing yourself in Merlin's Maze.

Then there's the junior karts, bumper boats, a climbing wall for you to scale and even F1 go-karts for the budding Michael Schumaker's amongst you!

Holywell Bay, Newquay

INDOOR POOLS

Carn Brae Leisure Centre,
Redruth, Tel (01209) 714766

Dragon Leisure Centre,
Bodmin, Tel (01208) 75715

Lux Park Leisure Centre,
Liskeard, Tel (01579) 342544

Polkyth Recreation Centre,
St Austell, Tel (01726) 61585

Saltash Leisure Centre,
Saltash, Tel (01752) 840940

Ships & Castles Leisure Pool,
Falmouth, Tel (01326) 212129

The Splash Leisure Pool,
Bude, Tel (01288) 353714

HORSE RIDING

There are nearly 50 horse riding stables in Cornwall. When you're on horseback, because you are that much higher off the ground, you will see things differently.

And because you're on a horse, wildlife will not scamper away as quickly as it would if you were walking or on a bike, the horse isn't a worry to them and as you're sitting on it, neither are you.

You can get details of where the different stables are from the local tourist board (see back page).

SPRINGFIELDS Fun Park & Pony Centre

At Springfields you can bottlefeed the animals and at the end of the day you can help unharness the ponies and take them to their field for a well earned rest.

There are the rabbits to feed and lots more to make your day really interesting.

Springfield Fun Park and Pony Cenre St. Columb Major Near Newquay.

MORE TO DO...

THE MINACK THEATRE

In the 1930's a woman called Rowena Cade decided to build a theatre in the back of her garden!

This theatre is now world famous for its' extraordinary and beautiful setting above Porthurno Beach and during the summer different plays and musicals are performed.

The Minack Theatre, Porthcurno, Nr. Penzance

SHIPWRECK, RESCUE AND HERITAGE CENTRE

Don't miss the chance to visit this centre and climb aboard a real lifeboat. What's more you will be able to see a huge collection of underwater equipment dating back to 1740 and treasures found in old shipwrecks.

Then walk through an underground tunnel where clay trucks were pushed out to the ships in the port.

Shipwreck, Rescue and Heritage Centre Charlestown.

The Arthurian Centre

Here you can visit the site of the Battle of Camlann where King Arthur and Mordred met, fought and died.

There are beautiful woodland and riverside walks that will take you to 'King Arthur's Stone' and a nature trail to follow.

Plus there's a children's play area with a wooden castle and the opportunity to do some brass rubbing.

The Arthurian Centre, Slaughterbridge, New Camelford

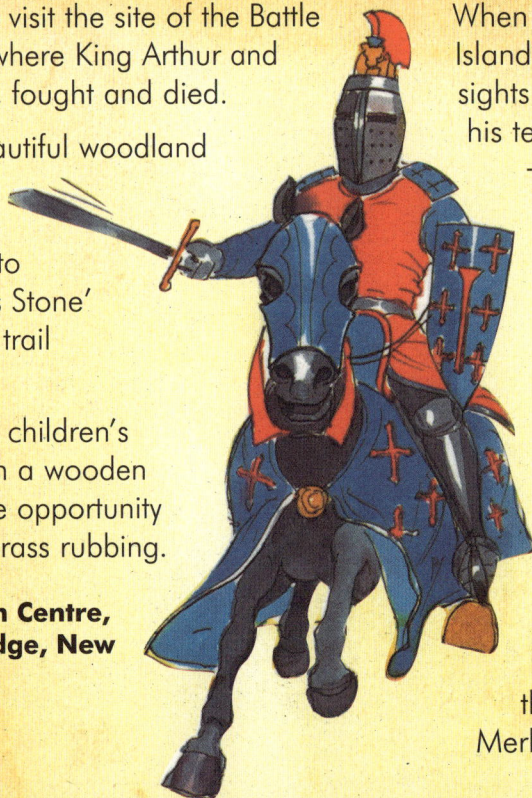

Tintagel Castle

When you explore Tintagel Island you will come across sights named after Arthur and his teacher Merlin.

There's King Arthur's Footprint, King Arthur's Seat, King Arthur's Cup and Saucer and even King Arthur's Bath!

Then underneath the Castle, on a finger of land that juts out into the sea, there's Merlin's Cave, which is said to be haunted by the ghost of the magician.

One story tells that it was here that the baby Arthur was washed into the cave on a huge wave and landed at Merlin's feet.

TAKE THE STEAM TRAIN

Cornwall has some great train journeys which will show you parts of the area that you would not normally see.

These journeys will take you aboard a wonderful old steam engine and you can become the 'Railway Children' for the day! So, All Aboard...

NARROW GAUGE RAILWAYS

LAPPA VALLEY STEAM RAILWAY

The Lappa Valley Steam Railway was opened in 1849 and runs on one of the oldest tracks in Cornwall.

As well as having an exciting ride on the trains you can also paddle a canoe, play crazy golf, have a lovely walk through the woods and even try to solve the puzzle of the maze.

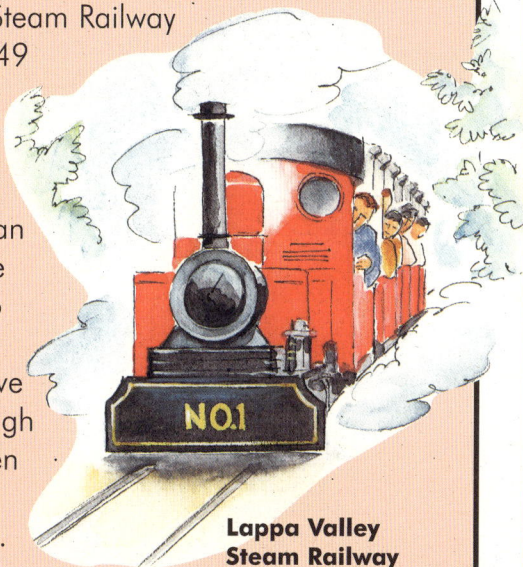

Lappa Valley Steam Railway St Newlyn East, Near Newquay

DOBWALLS ADVENTURE PARK

Here you will see the trains in the workshops and also get to have a great train ride through the forests.

Then there's a beautiful wood you can walk through where you can see all sorts of birds and wild flowers.

If that isn't enough there's a massive indoor play area with tube slides, ball pools and loads more. You can even get the chance to learn to drive!

Dobwell Adventure Park Near Liskard

LAUNCESTON STEAM RAILWAY

The train you will travel on is pulled by a locomotive built in Queen Victoria's reign. You can ride in an open or closed carriage so you can let the weather make your choice for you.

The guard will stop the train if you ask him at Canna Park or Hunts Crossing so you can get off and explore.

Back at Launceston Station there's the Transport Museum and Railway Workshops where you can find out more about the glorious days of steam.

Launceston

LOOE VALLEY LINE

This line has been running since 1879 and it will take you through nearly 13kms of wonderful countryside.

There are many interesting things to stop and see like the 2,000 year old stone circle at Duloe so it's worth getting off the train at one of the stations and exploring for a while before carrying onto your destination.

Looe Valley Line, (Looe or Liskard Stations)

BODMIN & WENFORD RAILWAY

There are three different stations you can get off at during this railway journey and at each of them there's a lovely nature walk, though if it's been raining you best have your wellies!

Bodmin & Wenford Railway, Bodmin General Station, Bodmin

WORLD OF MODEL RAILWAYS, Meadow Street, Megavissey.
Travel on miniature railways through a wonderful tiny world of villages starting your journey in an English town and ending up in the Swiss Alps!

MUSEUMS WITH SPECIAL INTEREST

MUSEUM OF WITCHCRAFT Boscastle

Amongst many other 'magical' items you can see a dead man's hand which people believed had very magical powers especially if it had been cut off from a hanged man!

As well as being used as a sort of medicine, burglars would make candles from the fat of the hand and the dried remains would be used as the candle holder!

It was called The Hand of Glory (gory more like!) and was supposed to make burglars invisible and people who saw them would be unable to move or speak.

NATIONAL MARITIME MUSEUM

A fabulous place to discover all about the sea, with brilliant 'hand-on' displays, a huge collection of boats to explore and tremendous sound and lighting shows.

Climb to the top of the 'Look-Out' and use the binoculars and telescopes to see for miles around. Then go down into the tidal zone where you'll actually be under the water.

Through two windows you can look into the harbour waters. Maybe you'll see a comorant diving after fish, or the bottom of a fishing boat as it sails past.

You'll learn about the sun and moon and how they effect the tides and interactive displays will introduce some of the plants and animals that live in the special conservation estuary.

National Maritime Museum, Discovery Quay, Falmouth

SMUGGLERS MUSEUM AND MR POTTER'S MUSEUM OF CURIOUSITY

Lots of exploring to be done here with three different places for you to visit.

There's the **Smugglers Museum** where you can find out about this secretive trade and a great sound and light show that explains it all in dramatic fashion.

Jamaica Inn was made famous by a writer called Daphne de Maurier and here you can find out more about her and the wonderful books she wrote.

Then there's **Mr Potter's Museum of Curiosity** where youll be amazed at the strange sights you will see. There are kittens enjoying a cup of tea, guinea pigs playing cricket and rabbits learning to read and write. Mr Potter was a taxidermist, that means he stuffed animals after they had died so as to preserve them.

Jamica Inn, Bolventor, on the A30 Launceston to Bodmin

MILITARY MUSEUM

With a collection dating back to 1704 this museum has a lot of very interesting things for you to see. There are medals and uniforms on display as well as other wartime memories that take you right up to the Second World War.

See also Bodmin Jail on page 15

Military Museum, The Keep, Bodmin

ROYAL CORNWALL MUSEUM Truro

A great place to visit to learn all about Cornwall's history right back to the Stone Age and up to the present day. The museum has an important bronze age collection of metal work, pottery, stone and flint tools.

There's even an Egyptian mummy for you to examine.

Royal Cornwall Museum, River Street, Truro

FOLK MUSEUMS

HELSTON FOLK MUSEUM

Everything you see here is to do with old crafts and industries that were part of life in Helston. There's a massive cider press, a complete Blacksmith's shop, farm wagons, a butchers cart and an old fire engine and much more to discover.

Helston Folk Museum, Old Butter Market, Heston

PORTHCURNO SECRET WARTIME TELEGRAPH MUSEUM – THE VICTORIAN INTERNET

You'll find this museum hidden among the cliffs. It was Cornwall's secret wartime communications centre where undersea cables fanned out from the beach to all parts of the Empire and beyond.

The tunnels, built in the Second World War, house a museum of historical equipment dating back to the 1870's.

Tintagel Toy Museum

Here you can see three generations of children's toys and they also have a collectors shop full of old and rare models.

BRITISH CYCLING MUSEUM, CAMELFORD

There are over 400 examples of cycles to see all housed in an old Victorian Railway Station. They have the first oil lamps used to light the way and a history of the cycle from 1818.

Automobilia

On the A35 Newquay to St Austell Road

There are over fifty collectors cars to be seen at this museum and you can watch an audio visual presentation that tells you about the history of the motor car.

THE WAYSIDE FOLK MUSEUM

This lovely museum actually lets you handle most of the exhibits so you can experience how they were used. There are blacksmith's tools, a range of exhibits and working water mills.

What's more you can do the museum quiz trail as you walk round and get a certificate at the end!

The Wayside Folk Museum, Zennor, B3306 road between St Ives and St Just

LANREATH FARM AND FOLK MUSEUM

You step right back in time when you visit this museum. In the kitchen there is one of the first ever pressure cookers and a washing machine that's nearly 100 years old.

There are old televisions, radios and then there's also some really old farm equipment.

Everything is set out in such a way that you feel that you've actually gone back in time.

Lanreath Farm and Folk Museum, Lanreath near Looe

HAVING FUN ON THE BEACH

Most of the beaches in Cornwall have lifeguards on duty during the holiday season. Even so you must always remember not to go in or near the water without an adult knowing where you are. Sometimes the sea looks calm but there might be currents or dips in the shoreline that could be dangerous. So, remember, have fun but be sensible and stay safe. Here are some games to play on the beach and a few puzzles that all have something to do with holidays by the sea.

WORDSEARCH

Not all the words run in straight lines. Some of them are L-shaped

A	B	Y	E	P	T	S	A	L
C	J	S	P	A	D	E	W	M
O	I	G	H	X	S	L	E	A
L	M	N	P	O	L	B	E	E
A	O	N	A	S	R	B	D	R
D	R	E	H	T	A	F	F	C
E	T	T	A	O	B	P	O	E
P	K	E	X	W	O	L	M	C
L	O	H	L	E	I	A	E	I
J	U	S	E	L	G	B	P	G
O	I	T	E	K	C	U	F	S

BUILDING SANDCASTLES

Use damp sand to build sand castles. Try filling different kinds of containers – like buckets, cups, biscuit tins and sandwich boxes to make really complicated castles.

Use pebbles and pieces of shells to decorate the walls.

To make flags for the towers and parapets: Use paper and sticks. But don't forget to take your rubbish home with you!

FOLD

GLUE TOGETHER

Make a different kind of sand construction by digging into the sand. Try digging a large, shallow hole in the shape of a boat. Leave a flat-topped ridge to sit on.

Sand sculptures can be of anything: people, animals, flowers, aeroplanes, volcanoes, islands... All you need is damp sand and your hands to mould it into shape. You may have to gently pour more water over the sculpture to keep it moist.

Remember to make sure your skin is always protected from the sun. You'll probably need to put more protection on after you've been in the sea.

SAND, PEDALO, FEATHER, SPADE, HAT, LILO, ICE CREAM, SEA, WEED, TOWEL, GAME, PEBBLE, BOAT, BUCKET.

SMUGGLERS' TUNNEL
Find the secret path through the Smugglers' Tunnel.

WORDSEARCH

Find the words under the magnifying glass. They may be spelt forwards, backwards, up, down, diagonally or in an L-shape. The word MORSE has been circled to help you. All the words have something to do with secrets and detectives.

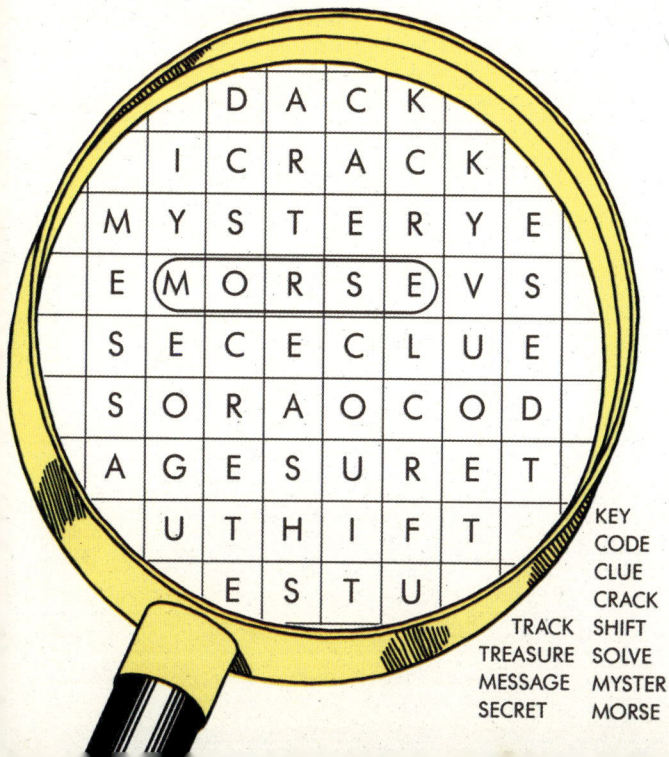

D	A	C	K		
I	C	R	A	C	K
M	Y	S	T	E	R	Y	E
E	M	O	R	S	E	V	S
S	E	C	E	C	L	U	E
S	O	R	A	O	C	O	D
A	G	E	S	U	R	E	T
U	T	H	I	F	T
E	S	T	U

KEY
CODE
CLUE
CRACK
TRACK SHIFT
TREASURE SOLVE
MESSAGE MYSTER
SECRET MORSE

LOOK AT THE PICTURE FOR 30 SECONDS, THEN COVER IT UP AND TRY TO ANSWER THE QUESTIONS AT THE BOTTOM OF THE PAGE.

How many rings were on the chest?
How many coins were on the chest?
How many bolts were on the chest?

MORE FUN...

SECRET HOLIDAY CODE

If you want your diary to be secret, write it in code. You can also send messages to your friends in code, and on postcards home. However, you'll have to give the person reading your note the Code-Cracking Card, unless you want them to spend a long time trying to work it out!

Here is a code called the "Number Code"

Write out the alphabet in one long line. Then write a number under each letter starting with 1 underneath A.

A	B	C	D	E	F	G	H	I	J	K	L	M	N	O	P	Q	R	S	T	U	V	W	X	Y	Z
1	2	3	4	5	6	7	8	9	10	11	12	13	14	15	16	17	18	19	20	21	22	23	24	25	26

To code a word use the number underneath the letter you need.

Try code the word HOLIDAY. It should look like this: 8, 15, 12, 9, 4, 1, 25.

To make it more difficult to crack you could use the shift number code. Pick a letter and give it the number 1. Write out the alphabet again and put the number 1 under the letter you have chosen. Then give the next letter in the alphabet the number 2 and so on until you have used all the numbers to 26. For example if D is given the number 1 it would look like this.

A	B	C	D	E	F	G	H	I	J	K	L	M	N	O	P	Q	R	S	T	U	V	W	X	Y	Z
24	25	26	1	2	3	4	5	6	7	8	9	10	11	12	13	14	15	16	17	18	19	20	21	22	23

CODE CRACKING CARD

This is how you make a Code-Cracking Card for the Number Code: Draw two circles, one smaller than the other, on a piece of card or paper. Cut them out. Put the smaller circle on top of the bigger one and put a matchstick though the centre of both of them. You should be able to turn the small circle without moving the big one. Write the letters of the alphabet around the outside of the bigger circle and numbers around the outside of the smaller circle, making sure the letters and numbers are exactly lined up. Remember, there are 26 letters in alphabet. Now turn the top circle four moves clockwise. The 1 should now be under the D and the 2 under the E, etc.

Try to decode these words

You'll need to find the number on the bottom line or inner circle and then write down the letter above it.

1. 3, 18, 11
2. 26, 12, 1, 2
3. 16, 5, 6, 3, 17
4. 10, 24, 9, 9, 12, 15, 26, 24

NOUGHTS & CROSSES

This is a game for two people and it's exactly like ordinary noughts and crosses but this time one player has a pile of stones, and the other has a pile of sticks. (You'll need to collect five of each.) Draw a grid in the sand, and take it in turns to put down a stick or a stone. The winner is the first one to make a straight line.

FRISBEE GAME

Place two markers on the ground about 5 metres apart. Stand behind your markers. Throw the frisbee to each other and score a point for each catch you make.

HOLIDAYS

How many words of 3 letters or more can you make out of the word HOLIDAY

SPOT THE DIFFERENCE

How many differences can you see?

LOOKING INTO ROCK POOLS

For a close-up view of rock pool life, cut off the bottom of a plastic bottle, you should ask an adult to help you do this, and to finish stretch a piece of clear plastic over the cut-off end. Secure the plastic with an elastic band.

Dip the bottle into the water and look through the top end. Be careful not to fall in the pool, and always put any rocks you remove back in place, an ordinary stone may be some little animals house.

My Journal

_____
_____
_____
_____
_____
_____
_____
_____
_____
_____
_____
_____
_____
_____
_____
_____
_____
_____
_____
_____
_____
_____
_____
_____
_____

The holiday logbook is your special souvenir. Write in it what you do each day and draw pictures of all the new things you see. Use code (see page 42) if you want the diary to be secret. Save your tickets from bus trips, boat rides and other excursions. Cut out pictures from brochures, collect postcards or take photos. You can stick all these in your logbook. When you get home show the logbook to your friends and keep it in a safe place. It will be a treasure you can always find to remind you of your holiday in Cornwall

My Journal

_____
_____
_____
_____
_____
_____
_____
_____
_____
_____
_____
_____
_____
_____
_____
_____
_____
_____
_____
_____
_____
_____

How many times did you spot me in the book?

Answer [ ]

My Journal

_____
_____
_____
_____
_____
_____
_____
_____
_____
_____
_____
_____
_____
_____
_____
_____
_____
_____
_____
_____
_____
_____
_____
_____
_____
_____

MY GREEN DETECTIVE SCORE CARD

SPOTTING FLOWERS ....
SPOTTING BIRDS ....
SPOTTING BUTTERFLIES ....
SPOTTING SEALIFE ....
OTHER SCORES ....

YOUR TOTAL SCORE

0 – 10 NOT A BAD START BUT YOU HAVE SOME MORE EXPLORING TO DO.

10 – 20 YOU'RE ON THE RIGHT TRACK, KEEP YOUR EYES OPEN.

20 – 30 WELL DONE INDEED, YOU'RE ON YOUR WAY TO BECOMING A GREAT GREEN DETECTIVE.

ABOVE 30 MOVE OVER SHERLOCK HOLMES! YOU REALLY ARE AN EXCELLENT GREEN DETECTIVE.